James Johnstone, Sturla Porkarson

The Norwegian Account of King Haco's Expedition Against

Scotland, A. D. MCCLXIII

James Johnstone, Sturla Porkarson

The Norwegian Account of King Haco's Expedition Against Scotland, A. D. MCCLXIII

ISBN/EAN: 9783337324209

Printed in Europe, USA, Canada, Australia, Japan

Cover: Foto ©ninafisch / pixelio.de

More available books at **www.hansebooks.com**

Norwegian Account

OF

King Haco's Expedition.

𝔅𝔦𝔟𝔩𝔦𝔬𝔱𝔥𝔢𝔠𝔞 ℭ𝔲𝔯𝔦𝔬𝔰𝔞.

THE

𝔑𝔬𝔯𝔴𝔢𝔤𝔦𝔞𝔫 𝔄𝔠𝔠𝔬𝔲𝔫𝔱

OF

King Haco's Expedition

AGAINST

SCOTLAND

A.D. MCCLXIII.

*Literally translated from the original Icelandic
of the Flateyan and Frisian MSS.*

BY THE

Rev. JAMES JOHNSTONE, A.M.,

and edited

WITH ADDITIONAL NOTES

BY

EDMUND GOLDSMID, F.R.H.S.,
F.S.A. (Scot.)

PRIVATELY PRINTED, EDINBURGH.

—

1885.

INTRODUCTION.

~~~~~~~~~~~~

PRINTED "for the Author," the Rev. JAMES
JOHNSTONE, Chaplain to the English Embassy
at Copenhagen, in the year 1782, this translation
of the Norwegian account of King Haco's Expedition had become very rare, when, in 1882, Mr.
WILLIAM BROWN, of Edinburgh, issued a reprint, limited to 250 copies. It was handsomely
printed, but, alas! the opportunity of making the
book really interesting to the student of History
and the general reader—by adding a few Notes,
explanatory of certain obscure passages—was lost,
and only a well-printed, and slightly *inaccurate*.
reprint of the 1782 edition was given by Mr.
BROWN. Such an omission, especially after Mr.
HUGH TENNENT's excellent translation of the
passages in P. A. MUNCH's *Norske Folks Historie*

which relate to this interesting episode, was really unpardonable; and, therefore, I trust that my efforts, however poor, to supply the deficiency, may prove useful to all who are interested in the History and Archæology of Scotland.

Such Notes as I have thought it necessary to add are indicated by the initials " E. G."; all others are Mr. JOHNSTONE's own.

EDMUND GOLDSMID.

EDINBURGH, *14th Feb. 1885.*

PREFACE.

(1782.)

THE Editor, from some particular advantages he enjoyed, was encouraged to collect such inedited fragments as might elucidate ancient history.

He, lately, published "Anecdotes of Olave the Black, King of Man;" and now lays before the learned the Norwegian account of Haco's celebrated expedition against Scotland.

It was the Editor's intention to have given a succinct detail of the descents made by the northern nations upon the British Isles, but an increase of materials induced him to reserve that subject for a future work. At present, therefore, he thinks it sufficient to premise that the Æbudæ were, long, the cause of much dispute between

various kingdoms. They seemed naturally connected with Scotland ; but the superior navies of
Lochlin rendered them liable to impressions from
that quarter.

The situation of the Kings of the Isles was
peculiarly delicate ; for, though their territories
were extensive, yet they were by no means a
match for the neighbouring States. On this
account allegiance was extorted from them by
different sovereigns. The Hebridian princes considered this involuntary homage, as, at least,
implying protection : and, when that was not
afforded, they thought themselves justified in
forming new connexions more conducive to their
safety.

The Alexanders of Scotland having united
Galloway, then a powerful maritime State, to
their dominions, began to think of measures for
obtaining a permanent possession of the Hebrides
by expelling the Norwegians. The preparatory
steps they took were first to secure the Somerled
family, and next to gain over the insular Chieftains. Haco was no less earnest to attach every
person of consequence to his party. He gave his

daughter in marriage to Harald, King of Man ; and, on different occasions, entertained at his Court King John, Gilchrist, Dugall the son of Rudri,[1] Magnus Earl of Orkney, Simon Bishop of the Sudoreys, and the Abbot of Icolmkil.

All this, however, did not effectually conciliate the Somerlidian tribe. The Norwegian monarch, disappointed in his negociations, had recourse to the sword, and sailed with a fleet, which both the Sturlunga-saga and the Flateyan annals represent as the most formidable that ever left the ports of Norway.

It would be improper for the Editor to draw any comparison between the Scottish and Norwegian narratives ; he, therefore, leaves it to the discernment of the reader to fix what medium he thinks reasonable.

The Flateyan and Frisian are the principal MSS. now extant, that contain the life of Haco the Aged. The first belongs to the library of His Danish Majesty, the latter is deposited in the

---

[1] (Dugald M'Rory). In Gaelic, " Ruadh Righ," is the red king; whence Roderick, and in Scotch parlance, Rory. (Note to Tennent's Translation from *Det Norske Folks Historie*, p. 2).— E. G.

Magnæan Collection. Of them the Editor obtained copies ; and by the help of the one was enabled, reciprocally, to supply the imperfections of the other. He has since examined the originals themselves. The Fr. MS. relates the following anecdote of Missel, at the coronation of Prince Magnus A.D. 1261. During Mass Missel the Knight stood up in the middle of the choir, and wondered greatly at some ceremonies unusual at the coronation of Scottish kings. And when King Magnus was robed, and King Haco and the Arch-bishop touched him with the sword of state, the Scottish knight said, " It was told me that there were no knights dubbed in this land ; but I never beheld any knight created with so much solem-nity as him whom two noble lords have now invested with the sword."

The conjectures in my note on page 43 are confirmed by the following passage in the Fl. MS. " Then came there from the Western seas John the son of Duncan, and Dugall the son of Rudra ; and both of them solicited that King Haco would give them the title of king over the northern part of the Sudoreys. They were with the King all summer."

Antiquarians may be desirous of knowing something of the MSS. from which this work has been taken, therefore, it was judged not improper to subjoin the following account of them. The Frisian MS. is a vellum quarto of the largest size, in a beautiful hand, and the character resembles that which prevailed in the end of the thirteenth century. The book of Flatey is a very large vellum volume in folio, and appears to have been compiled in the 14. age. It contains a collection of poems; excerpts from Adam Brebensis; a dissertation on the first inhabitants of Norway; the life of Eric the Traveller; of Olave Trygvason: of St. Olave; of the Earls of Orkney; of Suerir; of Haco the Aged; of his son, Magnus; of Magnus the Good; of Harald the Imperious; of Einar Sockason of Greenland; and of Olver the Mischievous; it contains also a general chronology down to A.D. 1394, the year in which the MS. was completed. The work, from the life of Eric the Traveller to the end of St. Olave's history, inclusive, was writtten by John Thordrson the priest; the rest by Magnus Thorvaldson, also a clergyman. The initial letters, in some places, are

ornamented with historical miniature paintings.
In page 35 there is a representation of the birth of
Trygvason ; and, at the bottom of the leaf, there
is a unicorn and a lion.   217, An archer shooting.
272, Orme Storolfson carrying off a haycock.
295, Haldan the Black beheading the Norwegian
Princes ; one of them is represented on his knees,
dressed in a red cap, a short doublet, and in red
trousers reaching down to the middle of his legs.
310, Three men armed with swords and battle-
axes, despatching St. Olave at Sticklestadt ; at
the bottom of the page a man killing a boar, and
another fighting with a mermaid.   650, Haco
creating Sculi a duke.   Sculi is drawn with a
garland or coronet, and receiving a sword,
together with a book by which he is to swear.
Most of the figures in these paintings are depicted
in armour or mail ; their helmets are sometimes
conical, sometimes like a broad-brimmed hat ;
their defensive armour is generally a round target
and a two-handed sword. This venerable volume,
the noblest treasure of Northern literature now
existing, though written in a very small character,
and much abreviated, consists of 960 columns—
two to every page.

THE HISTORY

OF THE

NORWEGIAN EXPEDITION
AGAINST SCOTLAND.

MDLXIII.

———◄◎►———

$\mathbf{A}$T the time that King Haco[1] ruled over Nor
way, Alexander,[2] the son of William, King
of Scotland, was then King of Scotland. He was
a great prince, and very ambitious of this world's
praise. He sent, from Scotland in the Western
Sea, two bishops to King Haco. At first they
begged to know if King Haco would give up those
territories in the Hebrides,[3] which King Magnus

---

[1] This was Haco IV., the bastard son of Swerro.
He began to reign in 1207.—E. G.

[2] Alexander II.—E. G.

[3] Sudr-Eyiar (orig.) The Hebrides or Southern
Division of the Scottish Islands, so called in contra-
distinction to the Orkneys.

Barefoot had unjustly wrested from Malcolm,
predecessor to the Scottish King. The King said
that Magnus had settled with Malcolm what districts the Norwegians should have in Scotland, or
in the islands which lay near it. He affirmed,
however, that the King of Scotland had no sove-
reignty in the Hebrides at the time when King
Magnus won them from King Godred.[1] And
also that King Magnus only asserted his birth-
right. The commissioners then said that the
King of Scotland was willing to purchase all the
Hebrides from King Haco, and entreated him to
value them in fine silver. The King replied,
he knew no such urgent want of money as would
oblige him to sell his inheritance. With that
answer the messengers departed. From this
cause some misunderstanding arose between the
Kings. The Scottish Monarch, however, frequently renewed the negotiation, and sent many
proposals; but the Scots received no other explanation than what is here related.

MCCXLIX.

Alexander, King of Scotland, wished much for
possession of the Hebrides. He had often sent to
Norway to redeem them with money, and he did

---

[1] Godred Chrou-ban, *i.e.*, the White-Handed,
King of Man.

so this summer. But when he could not purchase those territories of King Haco, he took other measures in hand which were not princely. Collecting forces throughout all Scotland, he prepared for a voyage to the Hebrides, and determined to subdue those islands under his dominion. He made it manifest before his subjects that he would not desist till he had set his standard east on the cliffs of Thurso,[1] and had reduced under himself all the provinces which the Norwegian monarch possessed to the westward of the German Ocean.[2]

King Alexander sent word to John, King of the Isles,[3] that he wished to see him. But King John would not meet the Scottish king till four earls of Scotland had pledged their honour that he should return in safety whether any agreement was made or not. When the kings met, the Scottish monarch besought King John that he would give up Kiamaburgh[4] into his power, and three other

[1] Thursa sker (orig.), i.e., the giant's rocks, Thurso.
[2] Solunder-haf (orig.), the Northern Ocean. So called from the Soloe Islands near that promontory of Norway called Stad. That species of sea-fowl which frequent the Bass probably received their name from being more commonly found in the Solund Isles.
[3] Eogan (in Gaelic, Eoin) Earl of Argyll.—E. G.
[4] Kiarna-borg (orig.). Fl. MS. Kianaborg, from the Irish carn, a rock, and the Icelandic borg, a castle. This castle was situated on a rocky islet near Mull. Fordun calls it Carnborg.

castles which he held of King Haco ; as also, the
other lands which King Haco had conferred upon
him.   The Scottish king added, that, if he would
join him in good earnest, he would reward him
with many greater estates in Scotland, together
with his confidence and favour.   All King John's
relations and friends pressed him to assent.   But
he behaved well and uprightly, and declared that
he would not break his oath to King Haco.   On
this King John went away, and stopped not at any
place till he came quite north to Lewes.[1]

King Alexander, then lying in Kiararey Sound,[2]
dreamed a dream, and thought three men came to
him.   He thought one of them was in royal robes,
but very stern, ruddy in countenance, somewhat
thick, and of middling size.   Another seemed of
a slender make, but active, and of all men the
most engaging and majestic.   The third, again,
was of very great stature, but his features were
distorted, and of all the rest he was the most un-
sightly.   They addressed their speech to the king,
and enquired whether he meant to invade the
Hebrides.   Alexander thought he answered, that

---

[1] Liod-hus, *i.e.*, the residence of Liot.   It is not
unlikely that the isle of Lewes and the family of
M'Leod were so named from Liod, Earl of Orkney.

[2] Kiarareyiar, in the MSS. Kiarbareyiar, the island
Kiararey (Karera, opposite Oban), where Alexander died
suddenly, Jul. 8th, 1249.

he certainly proposed to subject the islands. The genius of the vision bade him go back, and told him no other measure would turn out to his advantage. The king related his dream, and many advised him to return. But the king would not, and a little after he was seized with a disorder, and died. The Scottish army then broke up, and they removed the king's body to Scotland. The Hebridians say that the men whom the king saw in his sleep were St. Olave, King of Norway; St. Magnus, Earl of Orkney; and St. Columba.

The Scotch took for their king Alexander, the son of King Alexander. He afterwards married the daughter of Henry, King of England, and became a great prince.[1]

MCCLXI.

In summer there came, from Scotland in the west, an archdeacon, and a knight called Missel,[2] as envoys from Alexander, King of Scotland. They shewed more fair language than truth, as seemed to King Haco. They set out so abruptly on their return that none wist till they were under sail. The king' dispatched Briniolf Johnson[3] in

---

[1] Alexander III. attained his majority in 1262 : he married Margaret, daughter of Henry III.—E. C.

[2] Perhaps the author means Frissel, afterwards Bishop of St. Andrews ; or Michael, viz., de Wemyss, who was ambassador to Norway, A.D. 1290.

[3] More properly, Brynjulf Jonsson.—E. G.

pursuit, and he detained them with him.   The
king declared that they should remain that winter
in Norway, because they had gone away without
taking leave, contrary to what other envoys did.[1]

In summer there came letters from the kings of
the Hebrides in the western seas.[2] They complained much of the hostilities which the Earl of
Ross,[3] Kiarnach, the son of Mac-Camal, and other

---

[1] Alexander complained of the treatment of his
ambassadors to Henry III. of England, who wrote on
the 23d of March 1262 to Haco on the subject.   The
ambassadors were released before 15th November of
the same year, as is proved by letters from Henry to
Haco, of that date, thanking him for sending them
home.—E. G.

[2] The letters referred to here were propably the
ones written by Dugal M'Rory. (See *Tennent's Translation.*)—E. G.

[3] Jarlin af Ros ok Kiarnakr son Makamals (orig.)
The text here is much vitiated.   The author might
have read in some Irish accounts, Jarl na Ross (William) M'Kerchar, M'Calom, *i.e.*, the Earl of Ross
(William) the son of Ferchard, the son of Malcolm.
This William MacErchart was a young hero, and is
corruptly called Macentagart by the Scottish historians.   Or, perhaps, three persons may be alluded to,
v z., the Earl of Ross, Kinneach—son (of Kintail),
and a MacCamal of Lochaw, all powerful chieftains
on the west coast of Scotland.   It is, however, not
impossible that Kiarnak was some ancient chieftain,
from whom a branch of the Grants was called Clan-
Chiarnach.   The Fl. MS. for Makamals reads Macha-
mals.

Scots committed in the Hebrides when they went out to Sky.[1] They burned villages, and churches, and they killed great numbers both of men and women. They affirmed, that the Scotch had even taken the small children, and, raising them on the points of their spears, shook them till they fell down to their hands, when they threw them away lifeless on the ground.[2] They said also, that the Scottish king purposed to subdue all the Hebrides, if life was granted him.

When King Haco heard these tidings, they gave him much uneasiness, and he laid the case before his council. Whatever objections were made, the resolution was then taken, that King Haco should in winter, about Christmas,[3] issue an edict through all Norway, and order out both what troops and provisions he thought his dominions could possibly supply for an expedition. He commanded all his forces to meet him at Bergen about the beginning of spring.

---

[1] I Skid (orig.). In the Fl. MS. istrid, *i.e.*, to war.

[2] The inhuman practice here described was common in those times. From the Landnamaboc we learn that Olver first discouraged this custom. We read, Olver did not permit tossing infants from spear to spear, as was usual among pirates, and was therefore surnamed Barna-Kall, or the protector of infants.

[3] Jol (orig.). The great brumal festival among the Scandinavians. Hence the Scotch word Yule, *i.e.*, Christmas

MCCLXIII.

Near the middle of Lent King Haco travelled
from Drontheim[1] to Orkadal, thence east through
the mountains[2] to Bahus,[3] and so eastwards to El-
far[4] to see Earl Birger,[5] according to an appoint-
ment that they should meet at Liodhus in Easter
week. But when King Haco came to Liodhus[6]
the Earl was already gone away, and so the King
returned north to Bahus.

King Haco arrived at Bergen on the day of the
invention of the Cross.[7] He remained there during the spring, and proceeded in his preparations
with great diligence. Prince Magnus,[8] having
given the necessary directions through Rygia-
fulke[9] concerning the expedition and the equip-

[1] Nid-ar-os (orig.), *i.e.*, the mouth of the river Nid,
now Drontheim.
[2] Dovrefield mountains.—E. G.
[3] Vikor (orig.), now Bahus, in Sweden.
[4] Elfa, the river at Gottenburg.
[5] An earl of Sweden, and father-in-law to Haco the
younger.
[6] Liodhusa, a town of Sweden, demolished A.D.
1268.
[7] May 3.
[8] The son of Haco.
[9] *i.e.*, the hilly country. Harald Harfager divided
his kingdom into several counties, each of which was
to fit out a squadron of ships on an emergency. The
counties were again divided into *skipreidor*, or smaller
districts, each of which furnished a single vessel properly equipped.

ment of the fleet, went to join King Haco. After that a great number of barons, and officers, and vassals, and a vast many soldiers, flocked in daily to the Capital.

King Haco held a general council near Bergen, at Backa.[1] There the numerous host was assembled together. The King then declared concerning the expedition, that this whole army was intended against Scotland in the western seas, and to revenge the inroads which the Scotch had made into his dominions. Prince Magnus begged to command this expedition instead of King Haco, who should remain at home. He thanked him in many courteous words; but he observed, that he himself was older, and had longer acquaintance with the western lands, and that, therefore, he himself would go this voyage. He, however, gave Prince Magnus full power to rule the nation in his absence. At this council he settled many regulations respecting the internal government of the country; and he granted to the yeomanry, that, while he was away, no Sheriff should decide on any cause, unless such cause was of the greatest necessity.

During this voyage King Haco had that great vessel which he had caused to be constructed at

[1] *i.e*, an eminence near Bergen.

Bergen. It was built entirely of oak, and con-
tained twenty-seven banks of oars.[1] It was ornamented with heads and necks of dragons beautifully
overlaid with gold.[2] He had also many other well-
appointed ships.

In the spring King Haco sent John Langlifeson
and Henry Scott[3] west to the Orkneys, to procure pilots for Shetland.[4] From thence John
sailed to the Hebrides, and told King Dugal that
he might expect an army from the east. It had
been rumoured that the Scots would plunder in
the islands that summer ; King Dugal, therefore,
spread abroad a report that forty ships were coming from Norway. And by this means he pre-
vented the Scotch from making a descent.

Some time before the king himself was ready,
he sent eight ships to the westward. The captains of these were Ronald Urka, Erling Ivarson,
Andrew Nicolson, and Halvard Red.[5] They continued some days out in the road, as the wind did
not favour them.[6]

---

[1] By banks of oars we are only to understand
benches for the rowers.

[2] This ship was called the " Christsuden."—E.G.

[3] Evidently a Scotchman.—E. G.

[4] The meaning of this sentence is that they were
to procure pilots for the Scottish Seas, who were to
join the expedition in Shetland.—E. G.

[5] Munch calls him Halvard Rand.—E. G.

[6] These ships were intended for the support of
Man.—E. G.

When the king had prepared his ship, he removed all his army from the capital to Eidsvags;[1]
afterwards he himself returned to the city, where
he remained some nights, and then set out for
Herlover.[2] Here all the troops, both from the
northern and southern districts, assembled, as is
described in the Raven's Ode,[3] which Sturla[4]
sung:—

I.

From the recesses of Finland,[5] bands,
keen for battle, sought the potent Ruler
of the storm of javelins. The boisterous
deep, that girds this earth, bore the ships
of the Protector of thrones west from the
streams of Gotelfa.[6]

King Haco mustered all his force at Herlover.
It was a mighty and splendid armament. The

---

[1] *i.e.*, Cape Bay, near Bergen.
[2] An island and excellent harbour near Bergen.
Munch calls it " Herdle-vaer."—E. G.
[3] The " Ravnsmual" of Storla Thordssoen.—E. G.
[4] A celebrated poet, uncle to Sigvat Bodvarson, who
attended Haco in this expedition, and from whom
Sturla probably had his information of facts.
[5] The most northerly province of Norway.
[6] Or Gota.—E. G.

king had many large and well-appointed ships, as is thus described :—

II.

No terrifier of dragons,[1] guardians of the hoarded treasure,[2] e'er in one place beheld more numerous hosts. The stainer of the sea-fowl's beak,[3] resolved to scour the main, far distant shores connected by swift fleets.

III.

A glare of light blazed from[4] the powerful, far-famed monarch, while, carried by the sea-borne wooden coursers[5] of Gestils,[6] he broke to[7] the roaring waves. The

---

[1] *i.e.*, no warrior.

[2] The Scandinavian scalds and mythologists often represented treasures as guarded by monsters, dragons, sea snakes, &c. This notion probably originated from the fabulous tales of those who trade to the Indies. An ancient author, speaking of Scythia, says—"Nam quum in plerisque locis auro & gemmis affluant, Gryphorum immanitate, accessus hominum rarus est."

[3] *i.e.*, Haco.

[4] Rather " upon."—E. G.

[5] *i.e.*, ships.

[6] Gestil, a famous sea-king or pirate.

[7] Dashed through.—E. G.

swelling sails, of keels that ride the surge,
reflected the beams of the unsullied sun
around the umpire of wars.

Some nights after King Haco had arrived at
Herlover, Ronald and Erling sailed out of the
bay with their squadron. Ronald was separated
from the rest at sea, and made for the Orkneys
with some of the ships. But Erling, and Andrew,
and Halvard steered south before Shetland, and
so to the west of Tharey-fiord,[1] and they saw no
land except Sulna-Stapa[2] west of the Orkneys.
Afterwards they sailed in to Scotland under Dyrness.[3] They went up into the country, and destroyed a castle, but the garrison had fled. They
burned more than twenty hamlets. Next they
steered for the Hebrides, and found there Magnus,
King of Man.

Three nights before the Selian[4] vigils[5] King
Haco set sail for the German Sea with all his

---

[1] Thareyiar-fiörd (orig.), perhaps a mistake for
Faroeyiar-fiörd. Torfœs read it Barreyiarfiord.

[2] Mr. Johnstone suggested that *Sulna Stapa* meant
Staffa. It is more probable, from its being stated to
be *west* of the Orkneys, that the Sulesker, a barren
cliff, is intended.—E. G.

[3] *i.e.*, the promontory of Deer, now Durnish.

[4] The Seljumannaka.—E. G.

[5] 7th of July.

fleet. He had now been King of Norway six-and-forty winters.[1] He had a favourable breeze; the weather was fair, and the armament beautiful to behold, as Sturlas relates.

IV.

The abyss returned the flaming gleam of war, darted from the bright glittering concave shields of the goddesses of battle.[2] This voyage, by the bands of the troubler of peace, through the sea that streams around the world, was unwelcome to the foe—they dreaded the exactor of rings.[3]

---

[1] The Norwegians computed by winters; the Scotch did the same, as we see by Winton's Chronicle :—
  "Thretty winters and four than
  Edan regnyd Max Gowran."
[2] Val-drosar (orig.), the Goddesses of Fate; or Valkyriæ, to whom armour was supposed sacred.
[3] i.e., tribute-ringa elldingon (orig.), bright rings. *Ringa* signify not only rings, or bracelets, but also money; for before the introduction of coinage into the north, very thick spiral gold wires were worn round the wrists of great men, who distributed bits to those who performed any signal service; and such a wire is still to be seen in the Royal Museum at Copenhagen. It is not always easy to discern when by *ringa* is understood ornaments for the fingers, bracelets, rings of investiture, or the current money of the times.

King Haco had a company particularly selected
for his own ship. There were on the quarter-
deck Thorlife, Abbot of Holm,[1] Sir Askatin,[2] four
priests, chaplains to the king, Andrew of This-
sisey, Aslac Guss, the king's master of the horse,
Andrew Hawardson, Guthorm Gillas n, and
Thorstein, his brother, Eirek Scot Gautson, with
many others. There were on the main-deck As-
lack Dagson, Steinar Herka, Klomit Langi,
Andrew Gums, Eirek Dugalson,[3] the father of
King Dugal,[4] Einar Lang-bard, Arnbiörn Suela,
Sigvat Bodvarson,[5] Hoskuld Oddson, John Hog-
lif, Arni Stinkar. On the fore-deck there were Sigurd, the son of Ivar Rofu, Ivar Helgason of Lofloc,
Erlend Scolbein, Dag of Southeim, Briniolf John-
son, Gudleik Sneis, and most of the king's chamberlains, with Andrew Plytt, the king's treasurer.
There were in the fore-castle Eirek Skifa, Thorfin
Sigvald, Kari Endridson, Gudbrand Johnson, and
many of the cup-bearers. In general, there were
four men on every half-rower's seat. With King
Haco, Magnus, Earl of Orkney, left Bergen, and

---

[1] *i.e.*, the islet, a monastery near Bergen.
[2] Afterwards chancellor of Norway.
[3] Probably the son of Dugal, the son of Somerled.
[4] The father of King Dugal was Rory, I suppose.
See Notes on pp. 9 and 18.
[5] Nephew to Sturla, author of the Raven's Ode.
He attended Haco in this expedition.

the king gave him a good galley. These barons were also with the king, Briniolf Johnson, Fin Gausson, Erling Alfson, Erlend Red, Bard of Hestby, Eilif of Naustadale, Andrew Pott, Ogmund Krekidants, Erling Ivarson, John Drotning. Gaut of Meli, and Nicholas of Giska, were behind with Prince Magnus at Bergen, as were several other sea officers who had not been ready. Many approved commanders were, however, with King Haco, and of whom mention hath been made.

King Haco, having got a gentle breeze, was two nights at sea, when he reached that harbour of Shetland called Breydeyiar Sound,[1] with a great part of his navy, as Sturla sings:—

V.

The leader of his people unmoored the ploughers of the ocean,[2] and raised aloft the expanded wings[3] of his sky-blue doves.[4] Our sovereign, rich in the spoils of the sea-snake's den,[5] viewed the retir-

---

[1] Bressa Sound, near Lerwick.—E. G.

[2] *i.e.*, ships.

[3] *i.e.*, sails.

[4] Bla-dufor (orig.), *i.e.*, blue pigeons. The Scalds frequently compared ships under sail to birds, horses, and other animals in motion.

[5] *i.e.*, gold.

ing haven from the stern of his snorting
steed,' adorned with ruddy gold.

King Haco remained in Bredeyiar Sound near
half a month, and from thence sailed to the Orkneys, and continued some time at Elidarwic,[3]
which is near Kirkwall.[3] There he declared
before his men that he would divide his forces,
and send one part south to the Firth of Forth[4] to
plunder. But he himself wished to remain in the
Orkneys with the largest ships and greater part of
the army. The vassals and retainers, however,
spoke against this scheme, and made it evident
that they would go nowhere unless with the king
himself; so this proposed expedition was dropt.

After St. Olave's wake[5] King Haco, leaving
Elidarwic, sailed south before the Mull[6] of Ronaldsha with all his navy. At this place King
Haco was joined by Ronald from the Orkneys,
with the ships that had followed him. King Haco
next led the whole armament into Ronaldsvo, and
lay there for some space. He then sent men over

' *i.e.*, ship.
[2] The present Elweck.—E. G.
[3] Kirkio-vog (orig.), *i.e.*, Church Bay. Kirkwall.
[4] Breida-fiardar (orig.), *i.e*, Broad Bay. The Firth
of Forth.—*Johnstone.* Munch takes it to be the
Murray Firth.—E. G.
[5] St. Olave's Day, July 29.
[6] Mula in Irish and Icelandic signifies a cape or beak.

to Cathness[1] to levy contribution. He, on the
one hand, proposed peace if the inhabitants would
yield, but otherwise heavy punishment. The
Cathnesians submitted to the tax, and King Haco
appointed collectors to receive it, as is here inti-
mated.

VI.

First our wise sovereign, the bestower
of peace, and defender of the northern
thrones, imposed tribute, the ransom of
life, on the dweller of the Ness.[2] All its
tribes were terrified by the steel-clad
exactor of rings,[3] and panic-struck at his
mighty power.

While King Haco lay in Ronaldsvo a great
darkness drew over the sun, so that only a little

---

[1] Kata-nes (orig.), i.e., the promontory of Cadtav or
Cathness. Cathness was particularly exposed to the
inroads of the Norwegians. On this acconnt great
numbers of the inhabitants retired into Murray and
the adjacent counties, where they were afterwards
known by the name of Clan-Chattan.
[2] i.e., the promontory, or Cathness.
[3] Baug-gerdar (orig.), i.e., imposer of rings. *Baug*
signifies anything circular, therefore, in compounded
words, it is not easy to discern when it denotes rings
or shields, &c. See Note on Ringa, p. 26.

ring was bright round the sun,[1] and it continued so
for some hours.[2]

On the day of St. Laurence's wake[3] King
Haco, having ordered the Orkney men to follow
him as soon as they were ready, sailed over Pentland Firth;[4] Earl Magnus, however, staid behind.
He was here informed that John Drotning[5] and
Kolbein Aslacson, with the ships expected from
the east, but which had been accidentally detained, were arrived in the islands. King Haco
then sailed with all his forces to a haven that is
called Asleifarvic,[6] from that to Lewes, so on to
Raasa, and from thence to that place in Skye
Sound which is called Callach Stane.[7] Here he
was joined by Magnus, King of Man, and the re-

---

[1] This statement proves how accurate is this
account of the expedition, as it has been calculated
that this Eclipse took place on the 5th August 1263,
at 1.40 P.M., and was perfectly annular in the latitude
of Ronaldsay. It also settles beyond doubt the year
of the expedition.—E. G.

[2] This eclipse happened on the 5th of August 1263.

[3] St. Laurence's wake or vigil, 9th of August.

[4] Cathness by the ancient Britons was called Pentîr,
i.e., the headland, whence the neighbouring firth had
its name.

[5] i.e., John the Queen, perhaps the ancestor of the
M'Queens.

[6] Asleifarvick (orig.). Fl. MS., Hals-eyiar-vic.

[7] i.e., the old woman's rock. Cailleach in Irish, and
Kerling in Icelandic, signify an old woman.

lations Erling Ivarson, Andrew Nicolson, and
Halward. He next proceeded to the Sound of
Mull,[1] and then to Kiararey, where King Dugal
and the other Hebridians were assembled with all
their troops. King Haco had now above an
hundred vessels,[2] for the most part large, and all
of them well provided both with men and arms.

While King Haco remained at Kiararey he
divided his forces, and sent fifty ships south to the
Mull of Kintire[3] to plunder. The captains appointed over them were King Dugal, Magnus,
King of Man, Briniolf Johnson, Ronald Urka,
Andrew Pott, Ogmund Krækidants, Vigleic
Priestson. He also ordered five ships[4] for Bute;
these were under the command of Erlend Red,
Andrew Nicolson, Simon Stutt, Ivar Ungi Eyfari,
and Gutthorm, the Hebridian, each in his own
ship.

---

[1] *i.e.*, the promontory. This island was so called
because, from its propinquity to the opposite shore, it
appeared like a cape. The old Venetian edition of
Pliny has "Mella xxv. mill. pass. amplior proditur;"
in the other copies it is "Reliquarum nulla," &c.
Hence the true reading appears to be, Reliquarum
Mulla, &c.

[2] The Scottish historians fix the number of ships at
140.—E. G.

[3] Ken-tîr, *i.e.*, the promontory or peninsula in Scotland, Kintire.

[4] Munch fixes the number at 15.—(See *Tennent's
Translation*, p. 24.)—E. G.

King Haco sailed afterwards south to Gudey, [1] before Kintire, where he anchored. There King John met him; he came in the ship with Bishop Thorgill. King Haco desired him to follow his banner, as he should do. But King John excused himself. He said he had sworn an oath to the Scottish King, and held of him more lands than of the Norwegian Monarch; he therefore entreated King Haco to dispose of all those estates which he had conferred upon him. King Haco kept him with him some time, and endeavoured to incline his mind to fidelity. Many laid imputations to his charge. King Haco, indeed, had before received bad accounts of him from the Hebrides, for John Langlifeson came to the king, while he was sailing west from Shetland, and told him the news, that John, King of the Hebrides, breaking his faith, had turned to the Scottish Monarch. King Haco, however, would not believe this till he had found it so.

During King Haco's stay at Gudey, an abbot of a monastery of Greyfriars waited on him, begging protection for their dwelling and Holy Church: and this the king granted them in writing. Friar Simon had lain sick for some time. He died at

---

[1] *i.e.*, God's Island. I take this to be Giga, or, as Fordon calls it, Gia, compounded of the Gaelic *Dhia*, God, and the Icelandic *ey*, an island.

Gudey. His corpse was afterwards carried up to Kintire, where the Greyfriars interred him in their church. They spread a fringed pall over his grave, and called him a saint.

About this time men came from King Dugal, and said that the Lords of Kintire, Margad[1] and Angus[2] (also proprietor of Ila), were willing to surrender the lands which they held to King Haco, and to order their dependants to join him. The king answered, that he would not lay waste the peninsula if they submitted on the following day before noon; if not, he gave them to understand he would ravage it. The messengers returned. Next morning Margad came and gave up everything into the king's power; a little after Angus arrived, and likewise did the same. The king then said that, if they would enter into articles with him, he would reconcile them with the King of Scotland. On this they took an oath to King Haco, and delivered hostages. The king laid a

---

[1] Who this Margad was does not appear from history, I believe.

[2] Angus, Lord of Kintire and Ila, was grandson and heir of Reginald, King of the Isles. His posterity succeeded to the county of Ross, and John, the second earl, A.D. 1449, gave to his brother, Hugh, the barony of Slate, &c. Lord M'Donald, Baron of Slate, is the direct male representative of Reginald.

fine of a thousand head of cattle on their estates.[1] Angus yielded up Ila also to the king, and the king returned Ila to Angus upon the same terms that the other barons in the Hebrides enjoyed their lands ; this is recorded in the Raven's Ode.

VII.

Our sovereign, sage in council, the imposer of tribute, and brandisher of the keen falchion, directed his long galleys thro' the Hebrides. He bestowed Ila, taken by his troops, on the valiant Angus, the generous distributor of the beauteous ornaments of the hand.[2]

VIII.

Our dareful king, that rules the monsters of the deep,[3] struck excessive terror into all the regions of the Western Ocean. Princes bowed their head in subjection to the cleaver of the battered helm ; he often

---

[1] According to Munch, the number was 1200 head of cattle.—E. G.
[2] *i.e.*, rings or bracelets.
[3] *i.e.*, ships.

dismissed the suppliants in peace, and dispelled their apprehensions of the wasteful tribes.

South in Kintire[1] there was a castle held by a knight who came to wait on King Haco, and surrendered the fortress into his hands. The King conferred this castle upon Guthorm Backakolf.

We must next speak of that detachment of the army, which the king had sent towards the Mull of Kintire to pillage. The Norwegians made a descent there. They burnt the hamlets that were before them, and took all the effects that they could find. They killed some of the inhabitants; the rest fled where they could. But, when they were proceeding to the greater villages, letters arrived from King Haco forbidding them to plunder. Afterwards they sailed for Gudey to rejoin King Haco, as is here said.

IX.

The openers of gushing wounds, undaunted of soul, proceeded in the paths[2] of the famed Getis,[3] from the south round Kintire. Our heroes, rousers of the

---

[1] Probably Donaverty.—E. G.
[2] *i.e.*, the sea.
[3] A celebrated adventurer or sea king.

thundering tempest of swords, glutted the swift, sable-clad birds of prey in Scotland.

The wind was not favourable. King Haco, however, made Andrew Pott go before him south to Bute, with some small vessels, to join those he had already sent thither. News was soon received that they had won a fortress, the garrison of which had capitulated, and accepted terms of the Norwegians. There was with the Norwegians a sea-officer, called Rudri.[1] He considered Bute as his Birth-right; and because he had not received the Island of the Scotch he committed many ravages, and killed many people; and for that he was outlawed by the Scottish king. He came to King Haco, and took the oaths to him; and with two of his brothers became his subjects. As soon as the garrison, after having delivered up the strong-hold, were gone away from the Nor-

---

[1] Rudri or Ruari is the Irish abbreviation of Roderic. The person here meant is, no doubt, the second son of King Reginald, and the same who, in a donation to the abbey of Sandale, is styled Rodericus de Kintire filius Reginaldi. This Roderic, it seems, besides Allan and Dougal, had another son, Angus M'Rorie, Lord of Bute, whose daughter and heiress Jean was married to Alexander, sixth Lord High Steward, grandfather to Robert II., King of Scotland. Robert, A.D. 1400, gave Bute to his son John, from whom the present family of Bute is lineally descended.

wegians, Rudri killed nine of them, because he
thought that he owed them no goodwill.   Afterwards King Haco reduced the island, as is here
said.

X.

The wide-extended Bute was won from the
forlorn wearers[1] of rings by the renowned
and invincible troops of the promoter of
conquest,—they wielded the two-edged
sword—the foes of our Ruler dropt, and
the Raven from his fields of slaughter,
winged his flight for the Hebrides.

The Norwegians who had been in Bute went to
Scotland, where they burned many houses and
several towns.   Rudri, proceeding a great way,
did all the mischief that he could, as is here
described.

XI.

The habitations of men, the dwellings
of the wretched, flamed.   Fire, the de-
vourer of halls, glowed in their granaries.
The hapless throwers of the dart,[2] fell
near the Swan-frequented plain,[3] while

---

[1] i.e., the Scotch.
[2] i.e., the Scotch
[3] i.e., the sea.

south from our floating pines ' marched a
host of warriors.

While King Haco was in the Hebrides, deputies
came to him from Ireland intimating that the
Irish² Ostmen would submit to his power, if he
would secure them from the encroachments of the
English, who possessed all the best towns along
the sea-coast. King Haco accordingly sent Sigurd
the Hebridean, with some fast-sailing vessels, to
examine on what terms the Irish invited him
thither.

After this King Haco sailed south before the
Mull of Kintire with all his fleet, and anchored

---

¹ i.e., ships.

² Irar. (orig.), i.e. Irish. As the native Irish had
suffered so much from the Scandinavians, it is im-
probable they would apply for assistance to the *Siol
Lochlin na beum.* We may therefore reasonably con-
clude that the people here mentioned were the
descendants of those Norwegians or Ostmen, who
long inhabited the eastern coast of Ireland, and founded
some of its best towns. A.D. 1201, those Ostmen
or Easterlings were still so considerable that, at a
recognition taken of the diocese of Limerick, the
arbitrators consisted of 12 English, and 12 Irish, and
12 Ostmen. Edward I. gave Gilchrist, William, and
John Gilmorys, with other Ostmen in the county of
Waterford, peculiar privileges ; and, by the rolls of
Edward II. they evidently subsisted as a distinct
people during the reign of that prince.—Munch is of
opinion, on the other hand, that they were descendants of the O'Loghlen or O'Neill races. —E.G.

for some time in Arran Sound.[1] Then there
came often Predicant, or Barefooted friars, from
the Scottish Monarch, to King Haco, to sound
him about a pacification between the two Sovereigns. At this juncture also King Haco set
King John at liberty; and bidding him go in
peace, wherever he would, gave him several rich
presents. He promised King Haco to do everything in his power to effectuate a peace between
him and the Scottish King; and that he would
immediately return to King Haco whenever he
desired him. Soon after King Haco sent Gilbert,
Bishop of Hamar, Henry, Bishop of Orkney,
Andrew Nicolson, Andrew Plytt, and Paul Soor
as envoys to treat about a peace with the King of
Scotland. They went to the Scottish Monarch,
and laid before him their overtures.[2] He received
them honourably, seemed inclined to a compromise,
and said that such terms of accommodation as he
would consent to, would be transmitted to King
Haco. The commissioners departed; and the
Scottish envoys arrived soon after. King Haco
had ordered that all the Islands to the west of
Scotland, which he called his, should be wrote
down. The King of Scotland again had named
all such as he would not relinquish. These were

---

[1] The Harbour of Lamlash.—E. G.
[2] Alexander was then at Norar, or New Ayr.—
E. G.

Bute, Arran, and the two Cumbras;[1] as to other
matters there was very little dispute between the
Sovereigns; but, however, no agreement took
place. The Scotch purposely declined any
accommodation, because summer was drawing to
a period, and the weather was becoming bad.
Finding this, Haco sailed in, with all his forces,
past the Cumbras.

Afterwards an interview in Scotland was agreed
upon for a reconciliation.[2] King Haco sent
thither a Bishop and a Baron; and to meet them
came some knights and monks. They spoke
much about an accommodation, but, at last, things
ended the same way as formerly. Towards the
conclusion of the day a greater number of Scots
convened from the country than the Norwegians
thought were to be trusted. They, therefore,
retiring to the ships, waited on the King, and told
him their opinion. The generality advised him
to declare that the truce was now ended, and to
give orders to plunder, as the army was very short
of provisions.

King Haco, however, sent one of his courtiers,
called Kolbein Rich, to the Scottish Monarch.
He carried with him the Articles of pacification
which the Scottish King sent to King Haco, and

---

[1] Kumr-eyiar (orig.), *i.e.*, the islands of the Cum-
brians, two small islands to the west of Scotland.
[2] At Kilbirnie.—E. G.

D

was commanded to bring back the proposals
which King Haco had sent to the King of Scotland.
He was besides to propose that the Sovereigns
should meet with all their forces and treat about
a peace. If that, by the grace of God, took
place, it was very well; but if it should turn out
otherwise, then Haco proposed to the King of
Scotland to fight, with their whole armies, and let
him conquer whom God pleased. The Scottish
Monarch seemed not unwilling to fight, but he
gave no explanation. Kolbein, therefore, returned
back to his Sovereign, who appeared but little
satisfied with his message ; as is mentioned in
the Raven's-ode.

XII.

The eastern hero great in command,
and ennobled by victory, repeatedly
offered the decisive conflict of javelins to
the enemy. The strangers, distrustful of
their strength, risked not the combat
against our magnanimous Prince, wielder
of the gleaming blade.

The truce was now declared to be totally
ended. The king accordingly sent sixty ships in to

Loch-Long.[1] They were commanded by Magnus,
King of Man, King Dugal,[2] and Allan, his
brother, Angus, Margad, Vigleik Priestson, and
Ivar Holm. When they came into the inlet they
took their boats, and drew them[3] up to a
great lake which is called Loch-Lomond. On
the far side round the lake was an Earldom called
Lennox.[4] In the lake there were a great many

[1] Skipa-fiörd in Icelandic, and Loch-Lhong, in
Gaelic, signifies the Bay of Ships.

[2] Allan and Dougal, his brother, were, I imagine,
the sons of Rudri (see the note on page 37). This
Allan we may suppose to be the same who, in Rymer's
Fædera, is called "Alanus filius Rotherici," who A.D.
1284 was one of the Barons that engaged to support
Margaret of Norway's title to the Crown of Scotland. Dugal was probably the predecessor of M'Dougal
of Dunoly, *i.e.*, Olave's Tower. The place might
receive this name from having been the residence of
Olave, the youngest son of Somerled, thane of Argyle.

[3] To avoid long or dangerous circumnavigations, it
was usual for the ancients to draw their light canoes
over isthmuses. Among the Greeks such places were
termed διολκοι, *i.e.*, dragging places, and there was
a very remarkable one near Corinth. By the Scotch
they were called Tarbats, from the Gaelic *turn* to
draw, and *baat* a boat. There is a Tarbat between
Loch Lomond and Loch Long, and one on Loch
Fyne.—E. G.

[4] Alwin M'Arkel, as appears from the Chartulary
of Glasgow, was created Earl of Levnach by Maol-
Coluim IIII., A.D. 1153.

islands well inhabited ;[1] these islands the Norwegians wasted with fire. They also burned all the buildings about the lake, and made great devastation, as Sturlas relates.

XIII.

The persevering shielded warriors of the thrower of the whizzing spear[2] drew their boats across the broad isthmus. Our fearless troops, the exactors of contribution, with flaming brands wasted the populous islands in the lake, and the mansions around its winding bays.

Allan, the brother of King Dugal, marched far over into Scotland, and killed great numbers of the inhabitants. He took many hundred head of cattle, and made vast havoc, as is here described.

XIV.

Our veterans fierce of soul, feeders of wolves, hastened their wasteful course through the spacious districts of the mountains. Allan, the bravest of mortals,

---

[1] No doubt the neighbouring inhabitants retired to the isles of Loch-Lomond in times of danger.
[2] i.e., Haco.

at the fell interview of battle, often wreaked
his fatal vengeance on the expiring foe.

Afterwards the Norwegians retired to their
fleet, and met with so violent a storm that it
dashed in pieces about ten of their ships in Loch-
Long.[1] At this time Ivar Holm was seized with
an acute disease, which occasioned his death.

King Haco, as was before written, still lay in
the Hebrides. Michaelmas fell on a Saturday ;
and, on the Monday night after, there came a
great tempest with hailstones and rain.[2] The
watch on the forecastle of the king's ship called
out, and said that a transport vessel was driving
full against their cable. The sailors immediately
sprung upon deck ; but the rigging of the trans-
sport getting entangled in the king's ship, carried
away its beak. The transport then fell aboard in
such a manner, that the anchor grappled the cord-
age of the king's ship, which then began to drag
its anchors. The king, therefore, ordered the
cable of the transport to be cut, which was accordingly done. It then drove out to sea, but the
king's ship remained stedfast, and continued un-

[1] October 1st and 2nd, 1263.—E. G.

[2] The same storm which had destroyed the ten
ships on Loch Lomond. E. G.

covered[1] till daylight. On the morning, the
transport floated with the tide, and, together with
a galley, was cast ashore on Scotland. The wind
gradually increasing, the crew of the king's ship
got more cables, and dropt a fifth anchor. The
king himself then took to his long-boat, and rowing
out to the islands, ordered mass to be sung.[2] The
fleet in the meantime was forced up the channel;
and the tempest that day was so furious that some
vessels cut away their masts, others ran aground.
The king's ship also drove into the Sound, tho'
seven anchors, including that taken from the
transport, had been used. They then let go an
eighth, which was the sheet anchor; the ship still
drove, but the anchors at length took fast hold.
Five vessels were cast ashore. So great was this
storm that people said it was raised by the power
of magic, and the quantity of rain was prodigious,
as is thus described :—

XV.

Now our deep-enquiring sovereign encountered the horrid powers of enchant-
ment, and the abominations of an impious

---

[1] i.e., without an awning.—JOHNSTONE. Munsch
gives it as "without yards," those of the king's ship
having been carried away by the transport.—E. G.
[2] As no human power could assist them.—E. G.

race. The troubled flood tore many fair
gallies from their moorings, and swept
them anchorless before its waves.

XVI.

A magic-raised watery tempest blew
upon our warriors, ambitious of conquest,
and against the floating habitations[1] of the
brave. The roaring billows and stormy
blast threw shielded companies of our
adventurous nation on the Scottish strand.

When the Scotch saw that the vessels had run
aground, they assembled together, and advancing
against the Norwegians, attacked them with missile weapons.[2] They, however, defended themselves gallantly under cover of their ships ; the
Scotch made several attempts, at different times,
but killed few, tho' many were wounded. King
Haco, as the wind was now somewhat abated,
sent in some boats with a reinforcement, as is here
mentioned :—

XVII.

The victorious breaker of gleaming

---

[1] i.e., ships.
[2] The Scotch army was encamped at Camphill,
between Kilbirnie and Largs.—E. G.

weapons, attentive of soul, then sent his bands to the hard-fought field, where breast-plates rang. Our troops, by the slaughter of the suspicious foe, established their monarch's fame, villified by the dwellers of the vallies.[1]

Afterwards the sovereign himself, attended by Thorlaug Bosi, set sail in a barge belonging to the Masters of the Lights.[2] As soon as the king's men approached the land the Scotch retired ; and the Norwegians continued ashore all night.   The Scotch, however, during the darkness, entered the transport,[3] and carried off as much of the lading as they could.   On the morning, the king with a numerous reinforcement came on shore ; and he ordered the transport to be lightened, and towed out to the ships.

In a little time, they descried the Scottish army, and it was so numerous that they supposed the King of Scotland was present.[4]   Ogmund Kræki-

----

[1] i.e., the Scotch.

[2] Kerti-sveina (orig.), i.e., Inspectors of the Lights, who were to see that the Norwegian palace was properly illuminated.   The office corresponded exactly to the Canhowllyd of the Welsh Princes.

[3] In the Fl. MS. the Norwegians are said to have entered the transport.

[4] This does not seem to have been the case ; the army being commanded by Alexander of Dundonald,

dants with his company was stationed on a hill.
The Scottish van skirmished with his men ; and,
their main body coming on, the Norwegians entreated the king, as they were anxious for his
safety, to row to his fleet and to send them help.
The king insisted on remaining on shore ; but they
would not assent to his continuing any longer so
exposed ; he, therefore, sailed out in a barge to
his ships at the Cumbras. The following barons
remained on land :—Lord Andrew Nicolson, Ogmund Krækidantz, Erling Alfson, Andrew Pott,
Ronald Urka, Thorlaug Bosi, Paul Soor. The
whole number of soldiers with them was eight or
nine hundred. Two hundred men were upon the
rising ground with Ogmund ; but the rest of the
troops were posted down upon the beach.

The Scottish army now advanced, and it was
conjectured to consist of near fifteen hundred
knights.[1] All their horses had breast-plates ; and
there were many Spanish steeds in complete
armour. The Scottish king had, besides, a numerous army of foot soldiers, well accoutred. They
generally had bows and spears.

The Norwegians on the hill, apprehensive of

Steward of Scotland, grandfather to the Walter
Stewart or Stuart, who married a daughter of Robert
Bruce, and founded the royal house of Stuart.—E. G.

[1] Fl. MS., five hundred. This is the most correct
estimate. Munsch puts the Scotch cavalry down at
600.—E. G.

being surrounded, began to retire in scattered parties towards the sea. Andrew Nicolson, observing this, came up to the rising ground, and desired Ogmund to draw off his men towards the beach, but not to retreat so precipitately as if he fled. The Scotch at this time attacked them furiously with darts and stones. Showers of weapons were poured upon the Norwegians, who defended themselves, and retired in good order. But when they approached the sea, each one hurrying faster than another, those on the beach imagined they were routed. Some therefore leaped into their boats, and pushed off from the land, others jumped into the transport. Their companions called upon them to return, and some returned, tho' few. Andrew Pott leaped over two boats, and into a third, and so escaped from land. Many boats went down, and some men were lost, and the rest of the Norwegians at last wheeled about towards the sea.

Here Ilaco of Steini, one of King Haco's household, fell. The Norwegians were then driven south from the transport, and were headed by Andrew Nicolson, Ogmund Krækidants, Thorlaug Bosi, and Paul Soor. There soon began a severe contest, tho' very unequal, as ten Scots fought against each Norwegian. Among the Scotch there was a young knight called Ferash,[1] equally

---

[1] Perus or Pherus (orig.), probably Fergus.—JOHN-

distinguished for his birth and fortune. He wore
a helmet plaited with gold, and set with precious
stones, and the rest of his armour was of a piece
with it. He rode gallantly up to the Norwegians,
but no other ventured. He galloped frequently
along the Norwegian line, and then back to his
own followers. Andrew Nicolson had now reached
the Scottish van. He encountered this illustrious
knight, and struck at his thigh with such force that
he cut it off,[1] through the armour, with his sword,
which penetrated to the saddle. The Norwegians
stript him of his beautiful belt.[2] The hardest

STONE. Munsch gives his name as Peter of Curry.—
E. G.

[1] A quotation from Giraldus's account of the Irish
will both illustrate this passage and the antient method
of fighting. " Utuntur—securibus quoque amplis,
fabrili diligentiâ optimè chalybatis, quas a Norwegien-
sibus et Oustmannis sunt mutuati. Unâ tantum
manu, et non ambabus, securi percutiunt, pollice
desuper manubrium in longum extenso ictu regente, a
quo nec galea, caput, in conum erecta, nec reliquum
corpus ferrea loricæ tricatura tuetur. Unde et in
nostris contigit temporibus totam militis coxam ferro
utcunque fideliter vestitam, uno securis ictu præcisam
fuisse, ex unâ equi parte coxâ cum tibiâ, ex altera
verò, corpore cadente moribundo. Lapides quoque
pugillares, cum alia arma defecerint, hostibus in con-
flictu damnosissimos, præ alia gente promptius, et
expeditius ad manum habent."

[2] Knights at their creation were invested with belts
ornamented with gems. See Malmsb., book 2, chap. 6.

conflict then commenced.   Many fell on both
sides, but more of the Scotch, as Sturlas sings.

XVIII.

Where cuirasses rung, our generous
youths, formed in a circle, prostrated the
illustrious givers of bracelets.   The birds
of prey were gluttonously filled with lifeless limbs.   What great chieftain shall
avenge the fate of the renowned wearer of
the Belt?

During the battle there was so great a tempest
that King Haco saw no possibility of bringing the
army ashore.   Ronald, and Eilif of Naustadale,
however, with some men, rowed to land, and
greatly distinquished themselves ; as did those
troops who had before gone out in their boats.
Ronald, in the end, was repulsed to his ships ; but
Eilif behaved most heroically.   The Norwegians
now began to form themselves anew ; and the
Scotch took possession of the rising ground.   There
were continued skirmishes with stones and missile
weapons ; but towards evening the Norwegians
made a desperate charge against the Scotch on
the hill, as is here recorded.

XIX.

The champions of Nordmæra's' Lord
saluted the stout, harnassed Barons, with
the rough music of battle. The train of
the supporter of thrones, courageous, and
clad in steel, marched to the din of clash-
ing swords.

XX.

At the conflict of corselets on the blood-
red hill, the damasked blade hewed the
mail of hostile tribes, ere the Scot, nimble
as the hound, would leave the field to the
followers of our all-conquering king.

The Scotch then left the eminence, and fled
where they could, away to their mountains. The
Norwegians perceiving this, retired to their
boats, and rowing out to their ships, luckily
escaped the storm. On the morning they came
back in search of the bodies of those who had
dropt. Among the dead were Haco of Steini,[2]
and Thorgisl Gloppa, both belonging to King
Haco's household. There fell also a worthy vassal

---

[1] A district of Norway.
[2] He was chaplain to King Haco.— E. G.

called Karlhoved, from Drontheim, and another vassal named Halkel, from Fiorde. Besides, there died three Masters of the Lights, Thorstein Bat, John Ballhoved, and Halward Buniard. It was impossible for the Norwegians to tell how many were killed of the Scotch, because those who dropt were taken up and removed to the woods. King Haco ordered his dead to be carried to a church.

Five days after, King Haco commanded his men to weigh anchor and to bring his ship close under the Cumbras. He was soon joined by the squadron which had been in Loch-long. On the fast day following, the weather was good, and the king sent some retainers ashore to burn the vessels which had been stranded ; that same day the king sailed past Cumbra to Melansey,[1] where he lay some nights.

Here he was met by the Commissioners he had sent to Ireland, who assured him that the Irish Ostmen would willingly engage to maintain his army till he freed them from the dominion of the English. King Haco was extremely desirous of sailing for Ireland, and, as the wind was not favourable, he held a Council on the subject, but the whole army was against this plan. He, therefore, told them that as he was short of provisions

---

[1] Melanzeiar (orig.) Fl. MS. Melas eyiar, perhaps the island of Lamlash or Ailsa.

he would steer for the Hebrides. The king then ordered the body of Ivar Holm to be carried to Bute, where it was interred.

Afterwards King Haco sailed past Melansey, and lay some nights near Arran, then proceeded to Sandey, and so to the Mull of Kintire, and at night he arrived north at Gudey; next he sailed out to Ila Sound, where he remained two nights. King Haco laid a contribution, rated at three hundred head of cattle, on the island, but part was to be paid in meal, part in cheese. Haco set sail again on the first Sunday of winter, and met a fog and a storm so violent that few of the ships could carry their sails. The king, therefore, made for Kiararey, and about this time messengers passed between him and King John, but to little purpose. Here the king was informed that his troops had made depredations in Mull, and that some of the Mull men, with two or three Norwegians, had been killed.

King Haco next sailed in to the Calf of Mull,[1] where he stayed some nights. There King Dugal and Allan, his brother, took leave of the king, who gave them those estates which King John formerly possessed—Magnus, King of Man, and other Hebridians had returned home before. He

---

[1] Mylar-Kalf (orig.). Among the Norwegians a small island adjoining to a greater was called its calf, as the Calf of Mull, the Calf of Man, &c.

gave Bute to Rudri, and Arran to Margad. To
King Dugal he gave the castle in Kintire which
Guthorm Backa-Kolf had besieged and taken dur-
ing the summer. In this expedition King Haco
regained all those provinces which King Magnus
Barefoot had acquired and conquered from the
Scotch and Hebridians, as is here narrated.[1]

XXI.

The Lord of Egda[2] soon recovered all
those territories on the Continent which
had been subjected by the Scottish tribes.
In the western regions none durst contend
with the offspring of Ingui.[3] His army,
like a gathering tempest, indicated desola-
tion to the dominions of his imperious
adversary.

King Haco, leaving the Calf of Mull, sailed to
Rauney.[4] Here he overtook Balti, a vassal of
Shetland, with those who had been sent to the

---

[1] A Scotch Record, the *Melrose Chronicle*, states that
King Haco said it was the hand of God, and not the
Scotch, that compelled him to retire. He alluded to
the storm that had so damaged his ships.—E. G.
[2] A subdivision of Norway.
[3] Yngua (orig.), one of Haco's predecessors.
[4] Raasa.—E. G.

Orkneys, and to whom a permission had been
given of returning to Norway. King Ilaco from
Kauney steered northwards. The wind being un-
favourable, he made for Westerford, in Sky, and
ordered the islanders to supply him with provisions.
Next he sailed past Cape Wrath,[1] and arriving at
Dyrness, there happened a calm, for which reason
the king ordered the fleet to be steered into Giaford.[2] This was done on the feast of the two
apostles, Simon and Jude,[3] which fell on a Sunday. The king spent the night there. On this
festival, after mass had been sung, some Scots,
whom the Norwegians had taken prisoners, were
presented to the king. The king detained one as
a hostage, and sent the others up the country, at
liberty, on giving a promise that they would return with cattle. On the same day it happened
that nine men belonging to Andrew Biusa's ship
went ashore to procure water, and an outcry was
soon heard from the mainland. The crew, therefore, immediately setting off from their ships,
found two men swimming, though badly wounded,
and took them on board; the other seven, un-
armed, and incapable of making any defence,
remained by their boat (which was left aground
by the tide), and were killed by the Scotch. The

[1] Hvarf (orig.), signifies an intervening ridge that
intercepts the prospect—Farohead.
[2] Giafiörd (orig.). Fl. MS., Goa-fiörd. Probably
Loch Eribol.—E. G.   [3] October 28.

F

Norwegians landing, carried away their dead ; and
the Scotch, in the meantime, fled to a wood. On
the Monday, King Haco sailed from Giaford after
having liberated the Scottish hostage, and sent
him ashore. The king in the evening reached the
Orkneys, and anchored in a certain Sound, to the
north of Asmundsvo,[1] from whence he, with the
greatest part of his fleet, steered for Ronaldsvo.
In passing over Pentland Firth, a terrible
whirlpool appeared, and in which a ship from
Rygia-fylke, with all on board, perished. John
of Hestby was driven through the straits, and
was very near being swallowed up in the gulf;
but, by the mercy of God, his ship was forced east
to the ocean, and he made for Norway.

While King Haco remained in the Orkneys the
most part of his troops sailed to Norway ; some
went with the King's permission, but others took
leave for themselves. King Haco, on his arrival
at the islands, had at first given out that he would
return immediately to Norway ; but, as it was a
long time before the wind favoured him, he determined to winter in the Orkneys. He, therefore,
named twenty ships that were to remain with him,
and dismissed the rest. All the vassals stayed
with him, except Eilif of Naustadale ; he sailed
home. Most of the gentry, however, continued
with their Sovereign The king then despatched
letters to Norway, concerning the necessaries he

[1] Asmundar-vogi (orig.), i.e., Asmund's Bay.

should want. After All Saints Day, the King
steered for Medalland¹ harbour; but spent one
day at Ronaldsha.

On the Saturday before Martimmas, King Haco
rode to the port of Medalland, and after mass he
was taken very ill. He was aboard his ship
during the night; but, on the morning, he ordered
mass to be sung on shore. He afterwards held a
council to deliberate where the vessels should be
laid up; and ordered his men to be attentive, and
see after their respective ships. Upon this each
captain took the charge of his own galley. Some
were laid up in the harbour of Medalland, and
others at Skalpeid.²

Next King Haco proceeded to Skalpeid, and
then rode to Kirkwall. He, with such officers as
dined at his table, lodged in the Bishop's palace.
Here the King and the Bishop kept separate
tables in the hall. each for his own retinue; but
the King dined in the upper story. He ordered
certain districts to furnish his nobility and household with provisions. Andrew Plytt had the
inspection of the king's table, and delivered out
to the courtiers, retainers, masters of the lights,
and other attendants, their usual allowance. After
the proper arrangements were taken concerning
the disposal of the fleet, the different captains
went whither their ships were laid up. The

¹ Probably some harbour of Mainland, one of the
Orkneys.   ² A cape of Pomona—Scapa.—E. G·

barons who remained at Kirkwall were Briniolf
Johnston, Erling Alfson, Ronald Urka, Erling of
Birkey, John Drotning, and Erlend Red. The
other barons repaired to their proper districts.

King Haco had spent the summer in much
watchfulness and anxiety. Being often called to
deliberate with his captains, he had enjoyed little
rest, and when he arrived at Kirkwall, he was
confined to his bed by his disorder. Having lain
for some nights, the illness abated, and he was on
foot for three days. On the first day he walked
about in his apartments; on the second, he attended at the bishop's chapel to hear mass; and
on the third, he went to Magnus's Church, and
walked round the shrine of St. Magnus, Earl of
Orkney. He then ordered a bath to be prepared,
and got himself shaved. Some nights after he re-
lapsed, and took again to his bed. During his
sickness, he ordered the Bible and Latin authors
to be read to him. But finding his spirits were
too much fatigued by reflecting on what he had
heard, he desired Norwegian books might be read
to him night and day; first the lives of saints, and,
when they were ended, he made his attendants
read the Chronicles of our Kings from Haldan the
Black, and so of all the Norwegian monarchs in
succession, one after the other. The king still
found his disorder increasing. He, therefore,
took into consideration the pay to be given to his
troops, and commanded that a mark of fine silver

should be given to each courtier, and half a mark
to each of the masters of the lights, chamberlains,
and other attendants on his person. He order ed
all the ungilt plate belonging to his table to be
weighed, and to be distributed if his plain silver
fell short. At this time also letters were wrote to
Prince Magnus concerning the government of the
nation, and some things which the king wanted to
have settled respecting the army. King Haco received extreme unction on the night before the
festival of St. Lucia.[1] Thorgisl, Bishop of Stav-
anger, Gilbert, Bishop of Hamar, Henry, Bishop
of Orkney, Abbot Thorleif, and many other learned
men were present ; and, before the unction, all
present bade the king farewell with a kiss. He
still spoke distinctly, and his particular favourites
asked him if he left behind him any other son than
Prince Magnus, or any other heirs that should
share in the kingdom, but he uniformly persisted
that he had no other heirs in the male or female
line than what were publicly known.

When the histories of all the kings down
to Suerer had been recited, he ordered the life of
that prince to be read, and to be continued night
and day. whenever he found himself indisposed
to sleep.

The Festival of the Virgin St. Lucia happened
on a Thursday, and on the Saturday after, the

---

[1] December 13. — JOHNSTONE.   St. Luke, according
to Tennent (Dec. 12th).—E. G.

King's disorder increased to such a degree that he lost the use of his speech; and at midnight Almighty God called King Haco out of this mortal life. This was matter of great grief to all those who attended; and to most of those who heard of the event. The following Barons were present at the death of the king, Briniolf Johnson, Erling Alfson, John Drottning, Ronald Urka, and some domestics who had been near the king's person during his illness. Immediately on the decease of the king, bishops and learned men were sent for to sing mass. Afterwards all the company went out except Bishop Thorgisl, Briniolf Johnson, and two other persons, who watched by the body, and performed all the services due to so illustrious a lord and prince as King Haco had been. On Sunday the royal corpse was carried to the upper hall, and laid on a bier. The body was clothed in a rich garb, with a garland on the head, and dressed out as became a crowned monarch. The Masters of the Lights stood with tapers in their hands, and the whole hall was illuminated. All the people came to see the body, which appeared beautiful and animated, and the king's countenance was as fair and ruddy as while he was alive. It was some alleviation of the deep sorrow of the beholders to see the corpse of their departed Sovereign so decorated. High Mass was then sung for the deceased. The nobility kept watch by the body during the night.

On Monday the remains of King Haco were carried to St. Magnus' Church, where they lay in state that night. On Tuesday the royal corpse was put into a coffin, and buried in the choir of St. Magnus's Church, near the steps leading to the Shrine of St. Magnus, Earl of Orkney. The tomb was then closed, and a canopy was spread over it. It was also determined that watch should be kept over the king's grave all winter. At Christmas the bishop and Andrew Plytt furnished entertainments, as the king had directed, and good presents were given to all the soldiers.

King Haco had given orders that his remains should be carried east to Norway, and buried near his father and relations. Towards the end of winter, therefore, that great vessel which he had had in the west was launched, and soon got ready. On Ash Wednesday the corpse of King Haco was taken out of the ground ; this happened on the third of the nones of March. The courtiers followed the corpse to Skalpeid, where the ship lay, and which was chiefly under the direction of Bishop Thorgisl and Andrew Plytt. They put to sea on the first Saturday in Lent ; but meeting with hard weather, they steered for Silavog. From this place they wrote letters to Prince Magnus acquainting him with the news, and then set sail for Bergen. They arrived at Laxavog [1] before the festival of St. Benedict. [2] On that day

[1] *i.e.*, Salmon Bay.   [2] March 21.

Prince Magnus rowed out to meet the corpse
The ship was brought near to the king's palace,
and the body was carried up to a summer-house.
Next morning the corpse was removed to Christ
Church, and was attended by Prince Magnus, the
two queens, the courtiers, and the town's people.
The body was then interred in the choir of Christ
Church ; and Prince Magnus addressed a long and
gracious speech to those who attended the funeral
procession. All the multitude present expressed
great sorrow of mind, as Sturlas says :—

XXII.

Three nights did the brave warriors,
the flower of chivalry, continue at Bergen,
ere they entombed their wise and glorious
prince. The breakers of tempered metals
stood crowding around the grave of the
ruler of the nation, while in their swimming eyes appeared no look of joy.   Then
commenced those bloody feuds which till
our days have reigned.

King Haco was buried three nights before the
festival of the annunciation of the Virgin Mary ;
and after the Incarnation of our Lord Jesus Christ
one thousand two hundred and sixty-three years.

www.ingramcontent.com/pod-product-compliance
Lightning Source LLC
Chambersburg PA
CBHW021525090426
42739CB00007B/783

* 9 7 8 3 3 3 7 3 2 4 2 0 9 *